DESERT MORNINGS: POEMS FROM THE COACHELLA VALLEY

Lucy Wilson

TRANSCENDENT ZERO PRESS
HOUSTON, TEXAS

PUBLISHED BY TRANSCENDENT ZERO PRESS
www.transcendentzeropress.org

ISBN-13: 978-1946460981
Library of Congress Control Number: 2018945335

Printed in the United States of America

Transcendent Zero Press
16429 El Camino Real Apt. 7
Houston, TX 77062

Front cover art by Alan Wilde, "Looking for Lunch," digital photograph.

FIRST EDITION

Also by Lucy Wilson

Poems from the Left Coast
Wind on Water: Poems on Healing Arts and Songs of Love
In Due Season: Essays on Novels of Development by Caribbean
   Women Writers

For My Teachers

and

In memory of Roland Bush,

a great teacher

Author's Note

By dedicating my third book of poems to my teachers, I am acknowledging my debt to all who taught me in school, especially Professor Alan Wilde, Professor Gus Nigro, and Sister Marlene Brownett, SHCJ. These three educators gave me the skills I needed to be a teacher, a scholar, and (late in my professional life) a poet. They also taught by example and served as models as I honed my classroom techniques. I have had other teachers too: colleagues who gave me advice during my 34-year career, academics in Caribbean and postcolonial studies who helped me find my scholarly niche, artists and poets whose encouragement means so much.

Several persons helped me adjust to the unfamiliar desert climate and taught me about the regional flora and fauna, monsoonal rains, and sandstorms some call Haboobs. Staff members at The Springs Health and Fitness Center help me to strengthen my "core" to better cope with Parkinson's. Still others have helped me to expand my circle of friends and gradually to think of the Coachella Valley as home. There are too many people to acknowledge individually, but you know who you are and I thank you.

I am especially grateful to the founder of Transcendent Zero Press, Dustin Pickering, who has given me the means to reach readers from as far away as Bangladesh.

The poems in this book are a testament to the warm reception my husband and I have received in the Coachella Valley. In addition to my poems, the book contains several passages from different sources including poetry, philosophy, spirituality, and yoga studies. I am attempting to enhance the reading of my poems by juxtaposing these brief passages from Lao Tzu, Rumi, Yeats, Nietzsche and others from whom, over the years, I have learned about life and human nature.

CONTENTS

The spirit of the valley never dies.
      It is called the subtle and profound female
The gate of the subtle and profound female
      Is the root of Heaven and Earth.

Wing-tsit Ching, trans. The Way of Lao Tzu (Tao-te Ching)

But if the mirage is the mind itself,
What is then perceived by what?
The Guardian of the World himself has said
That mind cannot be seen by mind.

Shantideva, The Way of the Bodhisattva.

Morning in the Coachella* Valley

Pre-dawn shadow world gives way
to eastern glow and birds in flight;
towering pine trees and regal palms
shimmer in reflected light.

On the surface of the swimming pool
local mountains and distant skies
repeat this morning ritual
mirrored in my eyes.

Hummingbird pauses by my ear
curiosity helping to dispel fear.
Shadows and solids are tied to illusion:
only hummingbird's kiss exposes delusion.
Since mind cannot be seen by mind
the harder we seek, the less we find.

*The Coachella Valley: a desert valley in Southern California which extends for approximately 45 mi (72 km) in Riverside County southeast from the San Bernardino Mountains to the northern shore of the Salton Sea.

Rain

After twelve hours of heavy rain

Aloe plants send up ecstatic stalks

Distant mountains glisten white with snow

Animals or Angels?

A hawk flew down into my yard
and sat beside the garden Buddha.
They spoke softly for a while, as old friends do,
then hawk flew off to catch finches for breakfast,
leaving a trail of bird bones and feathers.

Falcon, predator. Buddha, meditator.
Humans walk a fine line between animals and angels,
violence and victory over unruly passions.
Such gifts we had and squandered
that we make the angels cry.
They come from a land of so much love
to earth, where love is confused with lust,
possession, control, dependence.

Angels rarely fraternize with humans.
We can't understand such caring, such giving:
desire tempered with generous tears,
passion seasoned with amazement,
the longing to protect, the need to share,
acceptance, wholeness, wonder.

Every discoloration of the stone,
Every accidental crack or dent
Seems a water course or an avalanche,
Or lofty slope where it still snows
Though doubtless plum or cherry-branch
Sweetens the little half-way house [. . .]

William Butler Yeats, "Lapis Lazuli."

Desert in Winter

Kissed by new snow, high peaks
behind local mountains
look much closer than they are—
a frozen white world
high above us.

In a poem by Yeats,* three Chinese men
climb toward a tea house on the gentle slopes
of a scenic mountain range. How unlike
Yeats' etching in blue stone
are these austere granite piles
10,000 feet above the desert floor,
like Zen stones reaching up to heaven.

*"Lapis Lazuli"

Surya Namaskara (Sun Salute)

The dynamic marriage of breath and movement into a serpentine flow is what sets this system of yoga [Ashtanga] from other methods. [. . .] Feel the air move across your body as you move through space. Be free. Be light. Be joyful in the experience and expression of your personal practice.

David Swenson. <u>Ashtanga Yoga: The Practice Manual</u>.

Morning Prayer

Moon going home
as Sun gets ready to rise:
on the edge
the break
the cusp
the crack,
the start of day.

Deep breath
clean slate
new leaf
fresh start
starting over
by choice or chance
accident or design
with or without
in sunshine and rain
now and forever
forgiveness
communion:
Come together
right now.

Enemies of Empathy

Greed at the heart of "progress"
those who brush off others' pain like dandruff
those who want to make my life their business
privilege masquerading as God's will
hypocrites and haters
violence in all its guises
religions and philosophies that divide rather than unite
all who diminish our shared humanity
those who missed the evolution elevator:
first stop compassion
next equilibrium
third floor lingerie
top floor enlightenment.
Not a belief system
but freedom from pain, sorrow, fear--
living and loving at a higher level.

Another Way

I am the feminine principle
though you have called me many names.
I am spring showers, summer flowers
dreams at night, stars so bright
dancing girls, hidden pearls
lunar astrology, most mythology
even mystery but rarely history.

His story is only half the tale:
conquest, enslavement, oppression
testosterone-fueled aggression
reluctance to compromise
a culture that is based on lies.

There is another way:
intuitive, compassionate
adaptable, commensurate
with the human position
as the flowering of earthly evolution.

If men carried their offspring beneath their hearts
for three quarters of a year
would there be so many pointless wars,
would we let our children live in fear?

The Garden

Low door in a high wall,
half hidden by leaves,
afternoon sun warms your back
as you enter the garden.
You may want to stay here a while—
no one would object.

Follow the soaring songbird,
hear the sigh of butterfly wings,
sing with cicadas and
dance with dragonflies.
Watch as hummingbird
turns cartwheels in the air
careening like a ball of fire
through inner and outer space.

Life in the Desert (Haiku Series)

1.   Dinner with friends
     we left behind in LA:
     bittersweet repast.

2.   Suspended in space
     the hummingbird reminds me
     to fill the feeder.

3.   Under the water
     a silver-blue world awaits
     the swimmer's entrance.

4.   The morning after
     fine sand on every surface:
     Haboob* has been here.

5.   Sun rises somewhere
     out of sight—the world transformed
     by heat and light.

6.   Hummingbird shadow
     against the seven-foot wall:
     shadow and bird are one.

7.   Leaf and dirt blowers
     next door, smell of gasoline
     six fifteen a.m.

.
monsoonal sandstorm

And I thought of the albatross,
And I wished he would come back, my snake.
For he seemed to me again like a king,
Like a king in exile [. . . .]
And so, I missed my chance with one of the lords
Of life.

D. H. Lawrence, "Snake."

Mallards

Mallard and mate
have taken a liking to my swimming pool.
She found it yesterday
and returned at first light with him in tow.
I suggested that they use the pool next door
where no one lives or cares about
duck droppings in the water.
They tried it out but soon returned.

Ducks landing on pool surface
sound like water-filled beach balls
dropped from a high place
reminding us that all is essentially water.

Wingless water-filled vessels
without webbed feet,
we humans cannot descend from the sky
to land in lakes, streams or swimming pools.
The impact would burst our balloons
and send the contents flying,
staining the blue water crimson.

With envy and admiration
I welcome my sleek, shimmering new friends
and await arrival of the pool guy,
a hunter of ducks who worries that
this pair in my pool is the advance guard
of a squadron of revenge-seeking water fowl.

New Music

Do you hear my voice inside your head?
Can you see the photos I've attached
to this e-mail *de la coeur* ?

I feel your presence
in my heart,
in my head.

Adam and Eve
robbed us of the knowledge
of our true nature.

Dance with me, my love,
up above the tree tops.
We'll sit on chimneys
and watch the sun set in the west,
our essential selves mingling
in the crimson glow.

Haute Cuisine

Squamous Cell Carcinoma
sounds like an entree
at a fashionable eatery
dimly lit
seared seafood
a hair's breadth away
from raw.
Sounds like
sarcophagus
sycamore
sagacious
but it's not a tomb
or a tree
or keen perceptions developed
over the course of a lifetime.
It is the desert's reminder
to respect the sun.

Things I Have Learned since Moving to the Desert

The desert is not always 110 degrees and sunny.
Winter can be cold and wet.
"Haboob" or sandstorm leaves fine brown silt on outdoor furniture.
Windstorms can topple gas grills and umbrellas.
Left outside on summer days, wax candles melt and form
    greasy puddles.
Hot coffee left in the sun stays hot.
Summer mornings are magical.
Swimming pools, sun-warmed to nearly body temperature, turn cold
    overnight.
Summer ends that same night.
Desert sunlight promotes visionary experiences.
Birds of all kinds live in tall pines, palm trees, and desert willows.
Some desert insects are so big they qualify as small monsters.
Dragonflies and cicadas are beautiful bugs.
Lizards think that if they stand very still we won't see them.
A piece of cactus, chopped off and placed in the ground,
    becomes another plant.
Because Coachella Valley is surrounded by mountains,
    night arrives early.
The desert night sky is heavy with stars like diamonds
    on an old woman's hands.

Welcome to My Garden
For Greg Fain, Garden Designer

Starting early and sometimes still singing
at midnight, the birds of Rancho Mirage
rule the morning until dry heat and golden sunlight
penetrate the darkest corners, and Flora
takes her place beside the resident Buddha
on the seven-foot wall that surrounds the garden.

Prickly Pear bleeds milk
from protrusions like beaver tails, flat as pancakes
but big as serving platters. Cut one off
and place it in the ground, and soon you'll have
two Prickly Pears growing in your garden.
In spring this cactus trades its green housedress
for a robe of many colored flowers
reminding us that beauty is often found
in places inhospitable to humankind.
Verbena arrives at the ball wearing pastel pink and gold,
but Gardena's delicacy and intoxicating scent take home first prize:
the handsome prince and a love that never dies.

Aloe Vera's viscous fluid can sooth rough skin
and speed recovery from burns.
Gold and deep purple Fountain Grass
cascades over garden borders
and on to the path that circles the pool.
Wandering Jade vines spill out of pots
while Fire Sticks reach up like flames
to the cobalt sky above.
Candelabra Cactus, tall and slim,
produces at its highest point a single flower
that blooms one day and dies:
beauty and brevity in the beholder's eyes.

Hark! hark! the lark at heaven's gate sings,
  And Phoebus 'gins arise.
His steeds to water at those springs
  On chaliced flowers that lies;
And winking Mary-buds begin
  To ope their golden eyes:
With everything that pretty is.
  My lady sweet, arise:
  Arise, arise!

William Shakespeare. "Hark! Hark! the Lark." (Aubade.)

Meditations on a Theme: Salute to the Sun

Below my terrace
east-facing flowers
fill with light
turning yellow to gold
and pink to deepest coral.
A tiny airborne bird does backwards flips.
This is no ordinary bird:
self-immolating and self-renewing
in a single gesture.
I cannot see the rising sun
but sun's emissary sings morning light
into my soul.

      ***

Sunrise touches distant peaks
and rolls across the valley floor:
a silent tsunami of light and heat.

      ***

The morning sun
washes the world,
dew drops anoint us
and palm fronds
wave benediction
as we witness the return
of color, size, texture, contrast.

Darkness before and after:
celebrate light!

***

Petals and stem
I open to you at dawn
bask all day in your warm rays
then close at sunset to dream of your touch.

***

The sun is rising,
lady of the dawn,
time to get up and begin the day.
While others work and pray,
you swim through sunbeams,
float on shimmering streams,
and fly through time and space
like one accustomed to dancing with gods.

***

Each day she mourns me
though I am never far.
She is learning to hear my voice
in the cheeping, peeping, burbling sound
of morning in the desert,
and the humming roar of cicadas any time.

***

As the sun rises
my west facing windows
glow in reflected light.

Teaching is reflected light.
My teachers touch my students' lives
though they will never meet.
Transference. Transformation.
In what unfamiliar faces
will my light shine?

***

Like a tree full of cicadas chanting at mid-day
love transforms the quotidian
heightens awareness
and compels us toward a place
both in and out of time.
Withholding love is withholding life.

***

Like a desert rainstorm in August, our moments together are brief
monsoonal downpours that wash away doubt and fear. I could no more
refuse your love than I could forget to breathe. Your voice in my head
opens the floodgate, and I ride the crest of a tsunami straight into the
heart of light.

Wingless

Wingless I fly
blind I see with unfamiliar clarity
deaf I hear music in my soul.

Stillness is the heart of life.

Do you accept this gift
this burden
this opportunity to save a world hell-bent
on self-destruction?
Come my friend and
we will fly among the treetops and
dance with Others who
have walked this path.

Stillness is the soul of life.

Silent cicada
hummingbird at rest
assure us that our hearts know what is best.
If we can imagine unheard music
earthen flute at forest's edge
then others too will join in singing
Gloria in Excelsis Deo
Glory to goddess too
Glory to me and you
and to all who hear the whales' lament
sound of breaking ice and crashing cement
total ruination without explanation.

If you choose to accept this assignment
which calls for much more than realignment--
calls for a spiritual rebirth
in the arms of mother earth--
then take my hand
and here we'll stand
till human beings learn that the answer is love
whether here on earth, in hell or up above.

Stillness is the song of life.

Night Life

At night the tall palm tree appears to soar
above the shimmering pool,
slender trunk dividing the garden in half,
a high opening in the curtain of twilight,
a crack, a fissure, point of entry to a world
that thrives on our discards: shadow, background, inner life.

By day, like a reliable servant or devoted wife,
shadow defines solids, background supports foreground,
and inner life knows its place.
As night falls, inner and outer exchange places
opposites merge, gyres collide, and the universe expands its
boundaries on energy released by spinning binaries.

Background-turned-foreground
opens doors to imagination
which fills the space with new content,
images that vibrate with mental energy.
Thus viewer becomes artist and artist creates space for new visions.

Nocturne

I hear them though I cannot see them
as they canter down the service road behind the house
snarling, barking, crying like human infants.
Night creatures
zombie dogs
canids from hell
coyotes
red eyes aglow
drool drifting from bared teeth:
I am grateful for the seven-foot wall between us.

Was man, indeed, at once so powerful, so virtuous, and magnificent, yet so vicious and base? He appeared at one time a mere scion of the evil principle and at another as all that can be conceived of noble and godlike. "

Mary Shelley, <u>Frankenstein</u>

Feast on Me

Deceptive Christmas card
picturesque winter scene:
farmhouse, fields, fences, pale sky
snow on branches
children skate on black ice
near-clear to sandy bottom.

In my dreams
the ice is
communion host thin
brittle as frozen foliage
crowded as the deep sea
with monsters who try
not to reveal themselves
by sudden breaks
in the shining surface.

In their water world
off limits to air-breathers
monsters subsist
on hearts and souls.
I walk on wafer ice
while they eye me from below
while they wait for a foot,
a hand, to break through
while they wait
for my body
to fall through a crack.
Monsters feast
on me.

Brute beauty and valor and act, oh, air, pride, plume, here
Buckle! And the fire that breaks from thee then, a billion
Times told lovelier, more dangerous, O my chevalier!

G. M. Hopkins. "The Windhover."

Food Chain

Hawk flies
    between rising sun
       and pine grove
          his shadow growing larger
            as it passes over my pool
          where he seeks careless songbirds
       too focused on filling their bellies
    to see the shadow's
swift approach.

We ought to be able to stand above morality, and not only stand with the painful stiffness of one who every minute fears to slip and fall, but we should be able to soar and play above it! How could we dispense with Art for that purpose, how could we dispense with the fool? —And as long as you are still ashamed of yourselves in any way, you still do not belong to us.

Friedrich Nietzsche, Joyful Wisdom

Dancing with Myself

As long as we are ashamed
of any aspect of our being
we cannot enter the garden.
Few protest that we must stay longer.
We cling to life despite pain, sorrow, lies,
friends who betray our trust,
family secrets, anger that survives entire lives,
grudges that fester like cancers on the soul.

We are invited to celebrate
BE NICE TO YOURSELF DAY.
For 24 hours we are asked to love ourselves,
to engage with, smile at, laugh with ourselves.
In return the universe prepares to welcome us back.

Living with the Past

Why must the sins of the fathers
be visited upon their children
for generations?
What if the children say:
"We will not carry your albatross
around another day"?

Guilt and shame rarely contribute
to the attainment of higher consciousness.
Hatred and revenge drag down
predators and victims.
Disrespecting others' beliefs
degrades one's own.
Using religion, nationhood,
racial and ethnic differences
to justify murder and mayhem
is a fast train to Perdition.

Oppression of women is needed,
some say, to preserve racial "purity."
Massacres and genocides:
all's fair in love and war.
This land is your land—but not for long.

All aboard the Perdition Express,
no exceptions! For what is hell
if not brother against brother
and we are all brothers and sisters beneath the skin.

Great Spirit

I am older than life
older than death as well.
Think back to a time
before you sold your souls
for autonomy and agreed
to consciousness limited
by self and other.

Better to be like a flock of birds
that airborne becomes
something greater than the sum of its parts,
or the V of Canadian geese
communicating via nuanced calls,
or whales' haunting chant
as much at home in the deepest oceans
as in the farthest reaches of the galaxy.

Except for the point, the still point
There would be no dance, and there is only the dance.

T. S. Eliot. "Burnt Norton" in Four Quartets.

Gnosis *involves recognizing, finally, the limits of human knowledge.* [. . .]

Elaine Pagels, The Gnostic Gospels.

Other Deserts

California deserts pay no heed to state lines.
They blend with Arizona's and New Mexico's tumble weed
and cactus plants with roots in rocky soil
and mountains scratching heaven's floor.
Big sky, hot summer breeze
monsoonal downpours, flash floods
electrical storms, sandstorms
that coat patio furniture in fine silt:
life in the desert presents special challenges.

New Mexico's flat-top mesas
lure artists to Santa Fe
but Utah's Zion park defies language
and leaves us with a sense
of the mysterious universe that we inhabit.

Zion's otherworldly massive facades
of iron-rich red clay
are penetrated by the green-tinted Virgin River.
Like shifting Northern lights above Canada's central plains
Zion evokes the presence of divinity or visits by angels
or extraterrestrials. The hieroglyphics, we are told,
are random marks left by glacial activity.
But in the golden light of late afternoon
the random marks of midday start to shift and blend
and speak in a million languages and ten billion voices:
Beloved! Be loved! Begin the dance—
for there is only the dance!

Lovers

Lovers and love live for eternity
All else is borrowed, Brother, leave it be

Don't be in thrall to passing shows that fade
Embrace the thing that is of spirit made

Love gives you wings to fly up to that place
Beyond the hundred veils of airy space

To be born you must first renounce each breath
And on the journey turn toward that death

That blinds you to the world and to the "I"
That tells you, you are eternity's sigh.

Rumi. Trans. Farrukh Dhondy.

All We Need

Love changes the fabric of existence.
Lovers are tested by circumstances;
time and distance, age and illness,
but mostly the difficulty of living at a higher pitch.

Even when we have cleared a path to the children's playhouse
in the garden near the forest where Great Spirit lives,
even then there will be moments of self-doubt
and raw fear.

Love is not an end but a means.
Love can tell what is from what seems.
Love is the dance that keeps the world turning.
Love is the fire that keeps inner light burning.
Love is the language that everyone speaks.
Love is the answer that everyone seeks.

Wave to Me

Morning is my favorite time of day.
I greet the rising sun on my yoga mat
or meditation bench, sometimes a chair or bed .
Use whatever you need. All props are eligible
if they help unroll dawn's carpet of light and heat
from the desert through the mountains
to the ocean and the beach.

Picture that as you sit in gridlock on the 60 or the 10,
watching your youth slip away,
inhaling fuel fumes, dodging monster trucks
and speeding sports cars. Wave to me
from the other side of gridlock.

Paths

On a soft day in November
I walk the paths of the Living Desert,
home to animals great and small from Africa
and the Americas. I rest between the gazelles
and the cape thick-knee, a short distance
from the cheetahs whose single stride
can reach 25 feet because of compressed kinesthetic energy
and aerodynamic design. For the moment
there are no other humans in sight.
I think of you and your artist's soul,
your loving heart, your attitude of mild amusement
at life's unexpected turns,
and I thank the goddess for placing me in your path.

Water and Spirit

They were here before parking lots,
rude drivers, elderly pedestrians
before gated communities, golf courses, HOAs
and marijuana dispensaries
before billboards advertising
dentists and exotic dancers.
Hidden in full view, the Indigenous people
of the Coachella Valley have prior claim
to this desert which they celebrate
with bright lights atop the casino: *Agua Caliente*.
For non-natives the term is synonymous
with slot machines and all-you-can eat buffet.
But for the Agua Caliente Band of Cahuilla Indians,
who have lived here for 5000 years,
the sacred waters that became Palm Springs
have played a major part in tribal lore and ritual.
The draining of the aquifers to water golf courses
has spiritual implications.
The gamblers and the golfers do not know
that the springs are the entrance
to the Agua Caliente underworld.*

*For years, the rate of the water drawn from the aquifer has depleted natural levels, which is known as over-drafting of the aquifer. http://www.coachellacleanwater.org/

Garden Buddha

Not happy or sad
but watchful, eyes bright
with inner light that bubbles up
like hot water
from a desert spring.

Crescent

Do not fear the solstice moon, sliver of silver
like Tibetan singing bowl
or tulip open
to the sun
or a smile.

Be watchful.
Be mindful.
Don't chatter.
Look within
and find there
what you seek.

No excuses.
We all have
crosses to bear.
Help one another.
Compassion produces
immediate return on your investment.

Night

Beware of bats
flying low
over the swimming
pool. In summer
we suggest hats
after sunset.

Inner Light

Some days the desert light
seems brighter, deeper
as it reflects off
pine trunks and palm fronds
and olive branches.
Toward sunset the landscape
 glows with inner light.
Mountains tower above
capped with pink snow
and dappled by cloud shadows.

References

Ching, Wing-tsit. Trans. *The Way of Lao Tzu* (Tao-te Ching). Upper Saddle River, NJ: Prentice Hall, 1963. 110.

Eliot, T. S. "Burnt Norton" in *Four Quartets. The Complete Poems and Plays* 1909-1950. NY: HBW, 1971. 19.

Hopkins, G. M. "The Windhover." *Chief Modern Poets of Britain and America.* 5th ed. Vol.1 Poets of Britain. Eds. Sanders, Nelson, Rosenthal. NY: Macmillan, 1970. I-61.

Lawrence, D. H. "Snake." *Chief Modern Poets of Britain and America.* 5th ed. Vol.1 Poets of Britain. Eds. Sanders, Nelson, Rosenthal. NY: Macmillan, 1970. I-221..

Nietzsche, Friedrich. *Joyful Wisdom.* NY: Frederick Ungar, 1960. 147.

Pagels, Elaine. *The Gnostic* Gospels. NY: Vintage, 1981

Rumi. Trans. Farrukh Dhondy. NY: Arcade, 2017.

Shakespeare, William. "Hark! Hark! the Lark." (Aubade.) *British and American Poets: Chaucer to the Present.* Eds. W. Jackson Bates and David Perkins. NY: HBJ 1986. 152.

Shantideva. *The Way of the Bodhisattva.* Trans. The Padmakara Translation Group. Boston: Shambhala, 2008. 233.

Shelley, Mary. *Frankenstein.* http://etc.usf.edu/lit2go/128/frankenstein-or-the-modern-prometheus/2303/chapter-13/

Swenson, David. *Ashtanga Yoga: The Practice Manual.* Austin, TX: Ashtanga Yoga Productions, 1999. 15.

Yeats, William Butler. "Lapis Lazuli." *The Collected Poems.* Ed. Richard J Finneran. 2nd ed. NY: Scribner, 1996. 294.

www.ingramcontent.com/pod-product-compliance
Lightning Source LLC
Chambersburg PA
CBHW072039060426

42449CB00010BA/2346